Beverly Cleary

My Favorite Writer

Susan Ring

WEIGL PUBLISHERS INC.

Published by Weigl Publishers Inc.
123 South Broad Street, Box 227
Mankato, MN 56002
USA
Web site: www.weigl.com

Library of Congress Cataloging-in-Publication Data

Ring, Susan.
  Beverly Cleary / Susan Ring.
     p. cm. -- (My favorite writer)
Includes index.
Summary: A biography of American author Beverly Cleary, who is best known for her books featuring Ramona Quimby, plus a chapter of creative writing tips.
  ISBN 1-59036-030-3 (lib. bdg. : alk. paper)
  1. Cleary, Beverly--Juvenile literature. 2. Authors, American--20th century--Biography--Juvenile literature. 3. Children's stories--Authorship--Juvenile literature. [1. Cleary, Beverly. 2. Authors, American. 3. Women--Biography. 4. Authorship.] I. Title. II. Series.
  PS3553.L3914 Z885 2002
  813'.54--dc21

                                        2002005588

Printed in Canada
1 2 3 4 5 6 7 8 9 10 06 05 04 03 02

Editor
Jennifer Nault

Copy Editor
Heather Kissock

Design and Layout
Terry Paulhus

Photo Researcher
Tina Schwartzenberger

Contents

Beverly Cleary

MILESTONES

1916 Born on April 12 in McMinnville, Oregon

1922 Moves from Yamhill, Oregon to Portland, Oregon

1938 Graduates from the University of California at Berkeley

1940 Becomes a children's librarian in Yakima, Washington; marries Clarence Cleary

1950 First novel, *Henry Huggins*, is published

1955 Gives birth to twins, Malcolm and Marianne

1975 Receives the American Library Association's Laura Ingalls Wilder Award

1984 Wins Newbery Medal for *Dear Mr. Henshaw*

1988 *The Girl From Yamhill*, an **autobiography**, is published

1995 The Beverly Cleary Sculpture Garden opens in Portland, Oregon

Author Beverly Cleary is just as interesting as the characters in her children's books. Is it possible for someone who refused to read books as a little girl to become a best-selling children's author? It is possible, because Beverly Cleary did just that. As a young girl, Beverly disliked reading. However, with some help and encouragement, she soon became an **avid** reader. When she was young, Beverly noticed that there were not many books about ordinary children like herself. Many years later, she began to write funny books that children could **identify** with. Her characters are fun, "regular" children, much like her devoted readers.

Beverly Cleary writes children's books about everyday situations. One of Beverly's most popular characters is Ramona Quimby. She is a funny, bothersome, and brave little girl. Readers of all ages laugh out loud at Ramona's silly antics. Read on to find out more about the life and work of Beverly Cleary, one of the most popular children's book authors of all time.

Early Childhood

"When I write I do not think about writing for children. I write the stories that I enjoy telling and feel that I am most fortunate that children enjoy reading them."
Beverly Cleary

Beverly Cleary was born Beverly Atlee Bunn in McMinnville, Oregon. Chester and Mable Bunn, Beverly's parents, welcomed her into the world on April 12, 1916. Beverly's early childhood was spent living on the family farm in Yamhill, Oregon. Today, the Yamhill farm is a place that Beverly remembers with much fondness.

As long as she followed her father's rules of safety, Beverly could do whatever she liked on the farm. A curious and active child, young Beverly was always up to something. She spent her days playing around the apple trees and the hen house on the farm. In Yamhill, Beverly learned much about nature. Her father taught her the names of local wildflowers. Her mother would sometimes take a break from her busy day to bring Beverly on nature walks. They would wander through fields and orchards. They would often come across wild animals, such as deer.

Yamhill was one of the first areas to be settled in the state of Oregon.

Beverly's determination was as strong as her curiosity. She was also apt to take adults' words a little too seriously. One day, Beverly's father tried to give her a lesson in geography. Eager to teach her about planet Earth, he used an orange to demonstrate that the world is round. He traced an imaginary circle around the orange with his finger. He told Beverly that she could travel completely around the world and end up where she had started.

Several months later, when the Bunn family was enjoying a picnic in the outdoors, Beverly bolted across the field. Her father shouted after Beverly, asking her where she was going. She replied, "Around the world, like you said." Little Beverly was swiftly carried back home. Beverly Clearly has continued to show this determination and curiosity. In fact, these qualities can be found in many of the characters in Beverly's books.

Yamhill, Beverly Cleary's birthplace, is located in Oregon's orchard region. Fine wines are produced from the grapes grown in this area.

Growing Up

By donating books, townspeople helped Mable realize her dream to have a library in Yamhill.

One of Beverly's favorite pastimes was listening to her mother tell stories and read to her. Mable would read classic tales to her daughter, such as "The Three Little Pigs," and "Little Red Riding Hood." While Beverly enjoyed listening to stories, she did not enjoy reading them. She had a hard time learning to read. Also, finding books in Yamhill was difficult because the small town had no library. Beverly's parents could not afford to buy books, so Beverly's first picture books were magazine advertisements, such as Jell-O recipes.

More than anything, Beverly's mother wanted to have a library in Yamhill. She knew that having a library would provide the town's residents with great educational opportunities. By donating books, townspeople helped Mable realize her dream. Before long, the state of Oregon began donating books as well. Mable Bunn became the very first librarian of the town. Although she was busy, Mable continued to read to Beverly every evening. Today, Beverly is grateful for her mother's strong example and for passing on her love of books and reading.

As a young girl, Beverly found reading difficult. Today, she supports and encourages struggling readers.

It was very difficult for Beverly's family to make a living by farming. When Beverly was 6 years old, the Bunns sold the farm in Yamhill. They moved to Portland, Oregon. Beverly's way of life changed overnight. While Portland was a big city, it did not take long for Beverly to feel at home there. She enjoyed living on Portland's Klickitat Street. There were many more children living in her new neighborhood than there had been in Yamhill.

Before long, Beverly started Grade 1. She had been excited about going to school, but Grade 1 was not easy for her. Beverly still found reading a challenge. This made her fear school, especially reading. However, Beverly was determined to learn. By Grade 3, with much practice, reading became easier for her. Before long, Beverly started reading everything that she could find.

Inspired to Write

Beverly Cleary has always enjoyed storytelling. When she was young, her mother spent hours reading to her. Mable would read everything from fairy tales to newspaper articles to her daughter. Mable **fostered** a love of books in Beverly. Without her mother's influence, Beverly may never have gone on to write children's books.

Beverly Cleary attended public school in Portland, the largest city in Oregon.

By the time Beverly entered high school, she had become an avid reader. While books were a great escape, they could not shelter her from the effects of the **Great Depression** in the 1930s. Beverly's father lost his job as a guard at the local bank. The Bunns were barely able to provide for themselves.

Writing stories brought joy to Beverly during these difficult times. In high school, Beverly wrote a story called "The Diary of a Tree Sitter" for an English writing assignment. She took her mother's advice and made the story simple and funny. Beverly received an excellent grade. Her English teacher told her that she was a talented writer. Beverly's next story was published in the school paper. It was called "The Green Christmas." It was a funny story about a boy who fell into a river that was filled with green dye.

The Great Depression affected the Bunn family, along with many other Americans. In 1933, more than 15 million people in the United States were unemployed.

Favorite Authors

Beverly's negative feelings about reading changed when she was in Grade 3. Her mother gave her a copy of *The Dutch Twins*, written by Lucy Fitch Perkins. It told the story of twins, Kit and Kat Vedder, and their lives in Holland. After reading this book, Beverly began looking for more books to read. She loved the book *More English Fairy Tales* by Joseph Jacobs. Her mother had to take it away from Beverly at bedtime, or she would stay up all night reading. Beverly continued to enjoy fairy tales such as Andrew Lang's *Blue Fairy Book* and *Red Fairy Book*. She tried to read all the books in the fairy tale section of the library. Beverly enjoyed all kinds of stories, especially those with happy endings.

After Beverly graduated high school, she left home to attend college in California. She had always dreamed of going to college. Beverly studied at the University of California in Berkeley. While there, she made many friends and attended parties and dances. At one party, Beverly met a man named Clarence Cleary. Little did she know at the time that he would be her future husband. After Beverly graduated university, she studied to become a librarian. She decided to make a career out of her love of books and libraries.

In 1940, Beverly began working as a librarian in Yakima, Washington. Being a librarian brought Beverly into contact with many children. She began to notice a troubling trend. Many children, especially young boys, did not like reading the children's books on the library's shelves. They found many of the stories outdated and unbelievable. Children wanted to read books with characters just like themselves. Beverly began to wonder if she could write books that children found interesting.

■ Beverly studied French grammar and English **literature** at the University of California in Berkeley.

Learning the Craft

When she started working as a librarian, Beverly saw that there was a need for different kinds of children's books.

Beverly's writing skills began to develop at a young age. She gained early writing experience with school assignments. When Beverly was reading, she would always pay close attention to the things she liked and disliked in the story. These **observations** stayed in her memory, and they helped Beverly later in her writing career.

When she started working as a librarian, Beverly saw that there was a need for different kinds of children's books. Children did not seem to be interested in what was available. Beverly wondered why all the books written for children were based on unbelievable events and characters.

Beverly remembered that she had wanted to read funny books about regular children when she was a child. She had wanted to read books with characters like the children living on Klickitat Street. In high school, the school librarian told Beverly that she should write books of her own someday. This idea stayed with Beverly for a long time.

As a librarian, Beverly met many different children who inspired her to write.

When Beverly was in Grade 7, her class was given an assignment to write a short story. Beverly wrote an imaginative story about feeding her pet chicken to George Washington's soldiers. Her teacher praised her writing and read the story aloud to the class. This gave Beverly the confidence to continue writing.

Beverly attended Grant High School in Portland. She wrote articles for her high school newspaper and continued to excel at writing in her English classes. However, Beverly did not do much of her own creative writing. Most of the things she wrote were for school assignments. Beverly did not explore creative writing until much later in life.

Beverly's experience as a librarian inspired her to start writing children's books. Working around children allowed Beverly to see first-hand how they responded to different books.

Inspired to Write

Sometimes, writing can be a seasonal job. In high school, Beverly found that the sound of the rain would calm her and help her write. She would write pages and pages with little difficulty. Today, Beverly still feels an **urge** to write when rain or snow is falling. It should come as no surprise that the author begins most of her books during the winter.

Beverly Cleary's high school, Grant High School, is still educating students in Portland today.

Getting Published

B everly's most popular books were published when she was an adult. However, the first time that she was published, Beverly was just a young girl. She even received a prize of $2 for her story. A local store sponsored a children's writing contest. The contestants were instructed to write a story about an animal of their choice. Beverly chose to write about the beaver. As it turned out, she was the only person who entered the contest. This did not dampen Beverly's excitement over winning. She also learned a great lesson. Beverly learned that in order to accomplish anything, you have to at least try. She realized that many people talk about writing, but only a few actually sit down and write.

> "I recalled my own childhood reading, when I longed for funny stories about the sort of children who lived in my neighborhood."
> **Beverly Cleary**

The Publishing Process

Publishing companies receive hundreds of **manuscripts** from authors each year. Only a few manuscripts become books. Publishers must be sure that a manuscript will sell many copies. As a result, publishers reject most of the manuscripts they receive.

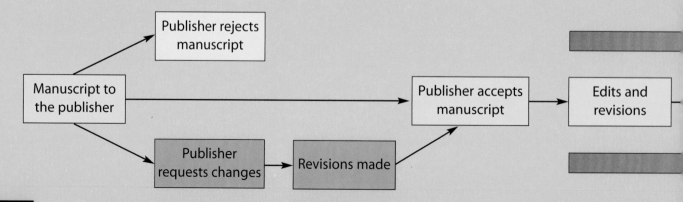

Many years after the contest, Beverly took her own advice and sat down to write. She felt inspired to write when she and her husband found a pile of typing paper in the closet of their new home. She began working on a book for children like those she met working as a librarian in Yakima.

Beverly Cleary was in her thirties when she wrote her first book. Writing a children's book was a wise decision. The book, called *Henry Huggins*, was about a boy from Portland. Beverly based the character of Henry on the regular children who came to the library. Luckily, the first publisher she sent the manuscript to accepted it. The publishing company was called Morrow Junior Books. *Henry Huggins* was published in 1950 and was an instant success. Before long, librarians, just like Beverly, were loaning out *Henry Huggins* to eager young readers.

Inspired to Write

Beverly Cleary's most popular book characters, such as Henry Huggins and Ramona Quimby, live and play around Klickitat Street in Portland. This is the same neighborhood where Beverly grew up. You can often find one of these characters popping up in different Beverly Cleary books.

Once a manuscript has been accepted, it goes through many stages before it is published. Often, authors change their work to follow an editor's suggestions. Once the book is published, some authors receive royalties. This is money based on book sales.

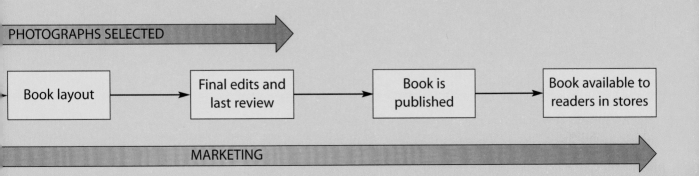

PHOTOGRAPHS SELECTED →

Book layout → Final edits and last review → Book is published → Book available to readers in stores

MARKETING →

Writer Today

The recent release of *Ramona's World* thrilled dedicated fans.

Over the years, Beverly has written more than thirty children's books. Today, Beverly Cleary and her husband Clarence live in Carmel, California, near the Pacific Ocean. When she is not writing, Beverly enjoys sewing and traveling. She also likes to read biographies and novels written by English authors. Beverly has two grown children, Malcolm and Marianne. They are twins. Marianne plays the cello for a living, and Malcolm works as a banker.

Beverly's most recent book, *Ramona's World*, was published in 1999. It is the latest addition to the popular Ramona series. These books are humorous tales about Ramona Quimby's many adventures. The recent release of *Ramona's World* thrilled dedicated fans. They were pleased to read about their favorite character again.

Beverly tells children that many of her ideas come from her own childhood experiences.

Since becoming a popular children's author, Beverly has traveled back to her home state of Oregon many times. When she visits Portland today, things look quite different. Even Grant Park, which is a few blocks away from where Beverly grew up, has changed. Grant Park now has statues of Ramona Quimby, Henry Huggins, and his dog, Ribsy. Along with the Clearys, more than 1,000 people attended the **unveiling** of the Grant Park statues in 1995.

In 1996, Beverly attended the unveiling of two more statues. Both are representations of one of her most popular characters, Ramona Quimby. These statues are housed in the public library in Gresham, Oregon. Sculptor Lee Hunt captured Ramona's lively, humorous personality in these life-sized figures.

On warm days in Portland's Grant Park, the fountains by the statues of Ramona and Ribsy are turned on.

Popular Books

Beverly Cleary has written books for all levels, from preschool to young adult. She has even written two autobiographies. Her autobiographies are called *A Girl From Yamhill* and *My Own Two Feet*. They are as delightful, funny, and interesting to read as her children's books. Above all, Beverly Cleary is known for her humorous books for children.

Henry Huggins

Henry Huggins is Beverly's first published book. It is about a young boy, Henry Huggins, who feels that his life is dull. He thinks that nothing exciting ever happens to him. This all changes when Henry comes across a stray dog on the street. Henry names the dog "Ribsy" because the dog is so skinny that his ribs stick out. Henry cannot leave poor Ribsy on the street, so he decides to take him home. However, getting home is more difficult than Henry had expected. Henry and Ribsy have many adventures along the way. Before the story concludes, readers are introduced to Henry's friends on Klickitat Street, including Beezus and her little sister, Ramona.

Beezus and Ramona

Henry Huggins has many neighborhood friends living around Klickitat Street. Beezus and her little sister, Ramona, are two of his friends. This book focuses on the relationship between these two sisters. Beezus finds her little sister **unbearable**. Ramona is always making trouble and getting all of the attention. Beezus struggles to deal with her mixed-up feelings for her irritating, yet adorable, little sister. When Ramona invites her entire kindergarten class over to her house without telling her mother, the trouble really begins.

Ribsy

Ribsy, Henry Huggins's dog, is the star of this humorous and delightful story. In this book, Ribsy gets hopelessly lost in a shopping mall parking lot. It is raining heavily, the pavement is slippery, and drivers are swerving to avoid him. Finally, Ribsy finds the Hugginses' car, jumps inside, and falls asleep. However, he has not jumped into his family car after all. Ribsy is taken to a different home, and a new family adopts him. Ribsy is heartbroken. He misses his owners and wants to find his real home. He especially wants to get back home to Henry. Ribsy's new owners call him "Rags." He does not like his new name. They also give him a bath, which is another thing Ribsy despises. Finally, Ribsy escapes. He has many adventures and causes many disruptions as he wanders around in search of Henry. He visits a classroom and joins a school football game. Will Ribsy ever find Henry? Readers will not be able to put this book down until they find out.

Ribsy is lost . . . and having the adventure of his life!

Louis Darling was the illustrator for most of Beverly Cleary's children's books, including *Ribsy*.

AWARDS
Ramona Quimby, Age 8

1982 Newbery
Honor Book

AWARDS
Ramona and Her Father

1978 Newbery
Honor Book

Ramona Quimby, Age 8

Ramona's humorous antics make for fun reading. At 8 years of age, Ramona feels like a grown up. She rides the bus on her own and looks after little Willa Jean after school. However, Ramona is having a more difficult time at school. The latest trend in the schoolyard is to crack a hard-boiled egg on your head. By mistake, Ramona's mother sends her to school with the wrong kind of egg. To Ramona's embarrassment, she winds up cracking a raw egg on her head. While waiting to get cleaned up at the school office, Ramona overhears her teacher call her a **nuisance**. Ramona is very hurt by this remark. She cannot erase it from her mind. How will Ramona handle this situation?

Ramona's World

Ramona's World is the most recent book by Beverly Cleary. Ramona Quimby is entering Grade 4. She expects it to be the best school year of her life, especially because she has a new best friend, Daisy. However, Ramona's year in the fourth grade turns out to be more complicated than she had expected. At school, she is teased by a **mischievous** boy that she calls Yard Ape. She is also having trouble in spelling. At home, she feels pressured by her parents. They expect her to be a good **role model** for the new baby in the family. On top of all that, Ramona's older sister, Beezus, is always receiving praise. Young readers will be amazed when they find out how Ramona turns her year around.

BEVERLY CLEARY
RAMONA'S WORLD

Ramona takes on fourth grade!

In *Ramona's World*, Ramona Quimby enters Grade 4 and turns 10 years old. She calls this her "zeroteenth" birthday.

Dear Mr. Henshaw

Leigh Botts is the new kid in town and is trying desperately to fit in. To make matters worse, his parents are recently divorced, and he has just lost his dog. Leigh is struggling to understand why his parents divorced. He is also living in a new neighborhood and trying to make a new life for himself. Leigh is upset at his father, who does not visit or telephone. Feeling very lonely, Leigh decides to write a letter to Mr. Henshaw, his favorite author. As he gets older, Leigh begins to write to "Dear Mr. Pretend Henshaw" in his diary. It gives him comfort and a place to express his feelings. This book deals with some sad issues, but it is a page-turner.

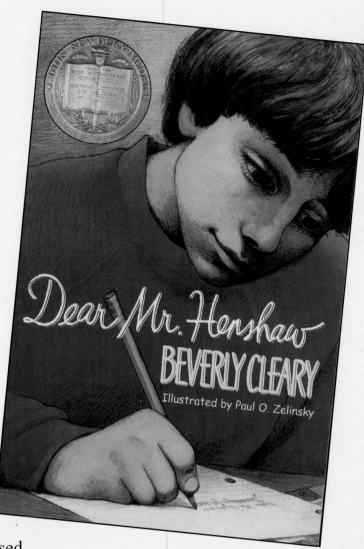

The Mouse and the Motorcycle

Malcolm, Beverly Cleary's son, loved motorcycles when he was in Grade 4. His interest served as the inspiration for the character, Ralph S. Mouse. Beverly wrote three adventure stories based on Ralph S. Mouse. The mouse lives in a hotel room, eating the crumbs left behind by the many families that have stayed in Room 215. When a family stays overnight at the Mountain View Inn, the young son, Keith, leaves a toy motorcycle in the hotel room. He does not know that Ralph, a talking mouse, lives in the room. Ralph discovers the motorcycle and goes for a spin. He ends up falling into the wastebasket by accident. Keith finds Ralph S. Mouse. Keith shows Ralph how to ride the motorcycle safely. While riding the motorcycle is fun, it is also dangerous. Will Ralph be able to stay out of harm's way?

AWARDS
Dear Mr. Henshaw
1984 Newbery Medal

Creative Writing Tips

T here are no strict rules for writing children's books. Every author has his or her own style and skills. The following are a few tips and **guidelines** that Beverly Cleary uses to help her write:

Make Writing a Habit

All skills get better with practice, including writing skills. Beverly Cleary suggests that to become a better writer, working every day is important. Begin by setting aside just 10 minutes a day to write, at the same time of day. This will help make a habit out of writing. By making writing a habit, writers will reach their goals with ease.

To Outline, Or Not to Outline?

Some authors need to draw up an entire **outline** before they begin writing. Not all writers work this way. Individuals have to discover whether using an outline works for them. Beverly Cleary feels that writing an outline does not work for her. In high school English class, Beverly learned how to use a story outline. She could create an outline, but she had trouble following it. Beverly felt that using an outline made her less creative. Still, for many writers, an outline is a useful tool. It helps them organize their ideas and stay on track during the writing process.

Beverly Cleary suggests that children who want to write should read many books.

Read, Read, Read

The more people read, the easier it becomes for them to learn about different styles of writing. Just as importantly, they get the opportunity to discover the kinds of books that they like and dislike. Beverly believes that reading is great preparation for becoming a writer. Children should read as many different kinds of books as they can find.

Tell A Story

A book is simply a story that has been written down. This is how Beverly views the writing process. Beverly imagines herself telling her story to an eager audience. She imagines the audience is sitting right in front of her. Then, Beverly writes down the words that she said to her make-believe audience.

Use Your Own Experiences

Fiction can be based on real people and events. Many of Beverly Cleary's ideas are drawn from her own childhood experiences. Adventures from Beverly's childhood remain clear in her mind, and she brings them to life in her writing. Her books are not completely autobiographical. Still, many of Beverly's childhood experiences can be found in her books. For instance, like Ramona, Beverly tied cans to her feet and walked around the neighborhood. She also had many adventures with her friends on Klickitat Street.

Inspired to Write

When Beverly's son, Malcolm, was in Grade 4, he became tired of books and reading. He only wanted to read books about motorcycles. Then, Malcolm became very sick with a fever. While he was recovering, the Clearys bought Malcolm a miniature motorcycle. This was the inspiration for The Mouse and the Motorcycle, which Beverly dedicated to her son.

Writing a Biography Review

A biography is an account of an individual's life that is written by another person. Some people's lives are very interesting. In school, you may be asked to write a biography review. The first thing to do when writing a biography review is to decide whom you would like to learn about. Your school library or community library will have a large selection of biographies from which to choose.

Are you interested in an author, a sports figure, an inventor, a movie star, or a president? Finding the right book is your first task. Whether you choose to write your review on a biography of Beverly Cleary or another person, the task will be similar.

Begin your review by writing the title of the book, the author, and the person featured in the book. Then, start writing about the main events in the person's life. Include such things as where the person grew up and what his or her childhood was like. You will want to add details about the person's adult life, such as whether he or she married or had children. Next, write about what you think makes this person special. What kinds of experiences influenced this individual? For instance, did he or she grow up in unusual circumstances? Was the person determined to accomplish a goal? Include any details that surprised you. A concept web is a useful research tool. Use the concept web on the right to begin researching your biography review.

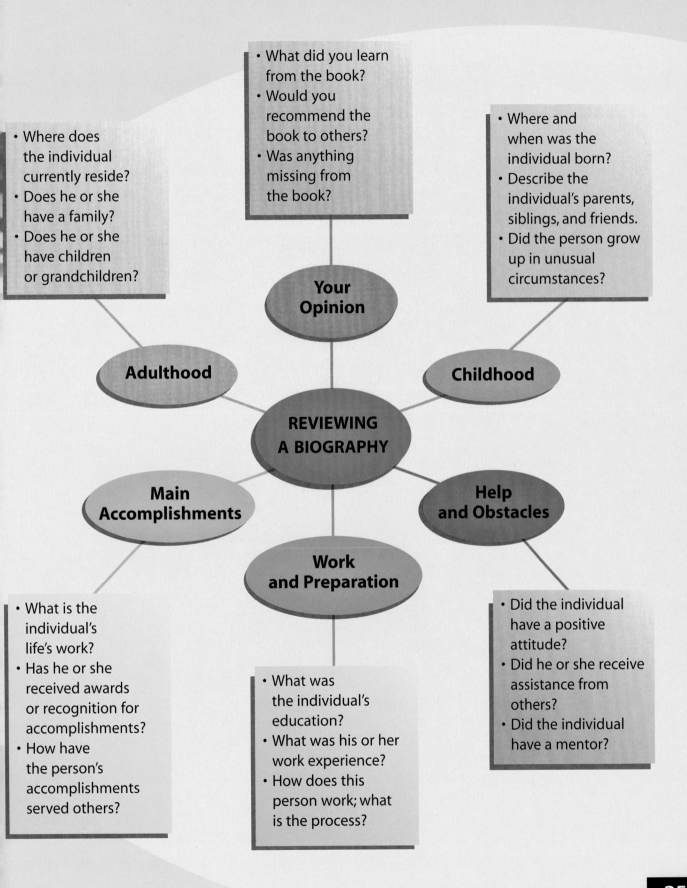

- Where does the individual currently reside?
- Does he or she have a family?
- Does he or she have children or grandchildren?

- What did you learn from the book?
- Would you recommend the book to others?
- Was anything missing from the book?

- Where and when was the individual born?
- Describe the individual's parents, siblings, and friends.
- Did the person grow up in unusual circumstances?

Your Opinion

Adulthood

Childhood

REVIEWING A BIOGRAPHY

Main Accomplishments

Help and Obstacles

Work and Preparation

- What is the individual's life's work?
- Has he or she received awards or recognition for accomplishments?
- How have the person's accomplishments served others?

- What was the individual's education?
- What was his or her work experience?
- How does this person work; what is the process?

- Did the individual have a positive attitude?
- Did he or she receive assistance from others?
- Did the individual have a mentor?

Fan Information

Beverly Cleary has won many awards for her outstanding writing and her lasting contribution to children's literature. In 1957, she won the Young Reader's Choice Award. She has also been given the Dorothy Canfield Fisher Children's Book Award. In 1984, Beverly was the United States author nominee for the International Hans Christian Andersen Award.

Beverly Cleary's books are available in more than twenty countries around the world. They can be read in fourteen different languages. Her books have been made into television programs in Japan, Sweden, and Spain. Television programs have been made featuring characters such as Ramona Quimby and Ralph S. Mouse. Many of these **adaptations** are still available in video stores.

Beverly Cleary has fans all around the world. Children continue to write to Beverly to tell her how much they love her books. Sometimes young fans suggest story ideas to Beverly. She has, at times, used some of her fans' suggestions in her books.

Beverly Cleary's books are available in more than twenty countries around the world. They can be read in fourteen different languages.

PBS aired a television special featuring Beverly Cleary's popular character, Ramona Quimby.

Ever since she wrote her first children's book, Beverly Cleary has gained many devoted fans. The Internet is a great place to find out more about the life of this fascinating author.

WEB LINKS

The World of Beverly Cleary

www.beverlycleary.com

This Web site offers a fun and lively look at one of the greatest children's authors of our time. Visitors can find information about their favorite Beverly Cleary characters. They can also explore a map of the neighborhood of Klickitat Street.

Multnomah County Library Kid's Page

www.co.multnomah.or.us/lib/kids/cleary.html

This is a great place to view the sculptures of Ramona, Henry, and Ribsy.

Quiz

1

Q: When and where was Beverly Cleary born?

A: Beverly Cleary was born on April 12, 1916 in McMinnville, Oregon.

2

Q: Where was the location of Beverly's family farm?

A: Yamhill, Oregon

3

Q: Where did Beverly's family move when she was 6 years old?

A: The family moved to Portland, Oregon.

Q: What university did Beverly Cleary go to upon graduating high school?

A: Beverly went to the University of California in Berkeley.

Q: What kind of work did Beverly do before she became a writer?

A: Beverly was a librarian.

Q: What is the name of Beverly's first children's book?

A: Henry Huggins

Q: What are the names of Beverly's twin children?

A: Malcolm and Marianne

Q: Where do Beverly Cleary and her husband, Clarence, currently reside?

A: Carmel, California

Q: On what street do the characters in many of Beverly Cleary's children books live?

A: Klickitat Street in Portland, Oregon

Q: What is significant about Grant Park in Portland, Oregon?

A: Grant Park has statues of some of Beverly's most popular book characters.

Writing Terms

This glossary will introduce you to some of the main terms in the field of writing. Understanding these common writing terms will allow you to discuss your ideas about books and writing with others.

action: the moving events of a work of fiction

antagonist: the person in the story who opposes the main character

autobiography: a history of a person's life written by that person

biography: a written account of another person's life

character: a person in a story, poem, or play

climax: the most exciting moment or turning point in a story

episode: a short piece of action, or scene, in a story

fiction: stories about characters and events that are not real

foreshadow: hinting at something that is going to happen later in the book

imagery: a written description of a thing or idea that brings an image to mind

narrator: the speaker of the story who relates the events

nonfiction: writing that deals with real people and events

novel: published writing of considerable length that portrays characters within a story

plot: the order of events in a work of fiction

protagonist: the leading character of a story; often a likable character

resolution: the end of the story, when the conflict is settled

scene: a single episode in a story

setting: the place and time in which a work of fiction occurs

theme: an idea that runs throughout a work of fiction

Glossary

adaptations: works produced in a changed form, such as a book for television

autobiography: a written account of one's own life

avid: very eager or enthusiastic

fiction: stories about characters or events that are not real

fostered: helped the growth or development of something

Great Depression: a period of economic hardship that lasted from 1929 to the 1940s

guidelines: information about how something is done

identify: to connect with, or understand, another

literature: writing of lasting value, including plays, poems, and novels

manuscripts: drafts of stories before they are published

mischievous: playful but troublesome

nuisance: someone who is naughty or a pest

observations: details that are noticed

outline: a summary of a story or piece of writing

role model: a person who serves as inspiration to others

unbearable: difficult to deal with

unveiling: a ceremony in which a new statue is shown to the public for the first time

urge: a strong desire

Index

Photo Credits

Cover illustration by Terry Paulhus
Archive Photos: page 10; Corel Corporation: pages 7, 9; courtesy of Grant High
School: page 13; courtesy of HarperCollins Publishers: pages 1, 4, 19, 20, 21, 27, 28; ©
Alan McEwen, 1999, courtesy of HarperCollins Publishers: pages 3, 16; David Falconer:
page 17; Map Resources: page 6; PhotoDisc, Inc.: page 8; Photofest: page 26;
PlanetWare, Inc.: page 11; Frances Purslow: pages 12, 22.